A Discourse, Delivered At Montpelier, October 17, 1834, Before The Vermont Colonization Society

William Chauncey Fowler

In the interest of creating a more extensive selection of rare historical book reprints, we have chosen to reproduce this title even though it may possibly have occasional imperfections such as missing and blurred pages, missing text, poor pictures, markings, dark backgrounds and other reproduction issues beyond our control. Because this work is culturally important, we have made it available as a part of our commitment to protecting, preserving and promoting the world's literature. Thank you for your understanding.

A DISCOURSE,

DELIVERED AT

MONTPELIER, OCTOBER 17, 1834,

BEFORE THE

VERMONT COLONIZATION SOCIETY.

BY WILLIAM C. FOWLER.

PUBLISHED BY THE SOCIETY.

MIDDLEBURY:
KNAPP & JEWETT, PRINTERS.
1834.

DISCOURSE.

The Question, WHAT SHALL BE DONE WITH THE COLORED POPULATION OF OUR COUNTRY? is one that has often been asked during the last sixty years; and as yet, it has received no answer, that has generally been satisfactory. Even before the United States, by the Declaration of Independence, assumed the responsibility of a distinct and separate national existence, there were intelligent patriots who made this question a subject of political speculation, or of christian solicitude. In the progress of time down to the present period, this solicitude has increased into a deep anxiety, and this speculation is maturing into speedy and decided action. The great mass of the population are waking up to the consideration of this subject; so that it may now be considered as morally certain that something will be done. An intelligent, conscientious, and enlightened people will act and must act.

But the question still recurs, *What* shall be done?

Now, to this, the AMERICAN COLONIZATION SOCIETY returns one answer; and the AMERICAN ANTISLAVERY SOCIETY another. The partisans of these two Associations are engaged in a fierce, or at least an animated controversy. They profess, and I doubt not sincerely, on both sides, to act in the name and by the authority of Jesus; and yet, to a considerable extent, the friends of each Association are endeavoring to prevent the operations of the other. Viewing the attitude in which they stand towards each other, and the spirit which has sometimes been manifested in the controversy, I could not but call to mind a certain passage in the Bible, in which the same spirit was manifested by the disciples and rebuked by Jesus.

In the Gospel by Mark, the ix. chap., at the 38th verse it is written—"AND JOHN ANSWERED HIM SAYING, MASTER, WE SAW ONE CASTING OUT DEVILS IN THY NAME, AND HE FOLLOWETH NOT US, AND WE FORBADE HIM BECAUSE HE FOLLOWETH NOT US. BUT JESUS SAID, FORBID HIM NOT."

I adopt this as the basis of my discourse, because it appears to be adapted to the present state of things in our country. The plain import of the passage is, that those who were casting out devils in the name of Jesus, received his approbation, even though they did not attach themselves to the disciples as to a party: They acted in the name and by the authority of Jesus, just as did the disciples, and therefore they ought not to be forbidden.

IT SHALL BE MY GENERAL PURPOSE TO SHOW, THAT EACH SOCIETY DOES, IN THE MAIN, ACT IN THE NAME AND BY THE AUTHORITY OF JESUS, AND THEREFORE SHOULD NOT BE FORBIDDEN. I shall,

I., speak briefly of the *history, condition* and *character* of the SLAVE POPULATION in our country.

II., of the *history, condition* and *character* of the FREE COLORED POPULATION. As related to these two classes, I shall speak,

III., of the *character* and *object* of the COLONIZATION SOCIETY: And,

IV., of the *character* and *object* of the ANTISLAVERY SOCIETY.

In the *first* branch of my discourse, I am to speak of the history, condition and character of the slave population.

It is now two hundred and fourteen years since slavery was first introduced into the territory of the United States. From a Dutch ship which had sailed up the James River, twenty slaves were sold to some Virginia planters. Little could those who bought, and those who sold these Africans, imagine what tremendous evils would grow out of a practice which they were thus introducing. This beginning of the system, which afterwards grew up, was but a speck in the horizon, which rose, and widened into a cloud of portentous blackness.

Owing to the encouragement offered to the traffic by the British Government, the business of importing slaves became a very extensive trade. Every one of the old thirteen States participated in the practice of slavery; the northern less indeed than the southern; not because their disposition was any better, but because their climate was not so well adapted to African habits and constitutions. The merchants and mariners of New England, engaged with their characteristic enterprise and activity in the transportation of slaves, for which their southern brethren furnished them with a ready market. The cheapness and fertility of the soil beneath those genial skies, and the correspondent high price of labor, which brought abundant returns to the planter; the small expense necessary for their shelter and clothing; the ease with which the art of growing tobacco, rice and cotton may be learned, made those states an inviting field for the employment of slaves.

And, what shows how easily the human heart is led into error, men learned to believe that by so doing they were bestowing a favor on their victims. Hawkins, the first Englishman who engaged in the traffic, when reprimanded for it by Queen Elizabeth, declared that "he considered it an act of humanity to transport men from a state of heathenism to the enjoyment of the christian religion;" just as if they would be converted to the faith of their oppressors by seeing the fruits of that faith in their own injury and sorrow. The planter too was ready to say, that he was performing an act of humanity, in rescuing men from the hold of the slave-ship; not considering that he was thus encouraging the multiplication of the very evil he was in a small degree endeavoring to relieve.

And not only planters and merchants who received a pecuniary benefit from the trade, but even philosophers and divines advocated the practice of slavery. Even Locke, that great master of reason, in the constitution which he formed for the Carolinas, introduced this declaration, that " every freeman of Carolina possesses absolute power over his negro slaves, of what opinion or religion soever."— Whitefield too, who preached so persuasively the gospel to the poor, left the authority of his name in favor of slavery, which he advocated on the ground of the great difficulty of procuring servants.

Men had not in those times learned what are the first principles of liberty. They practised slavery on the ground that it was permitted under the Jewish dispensation; forgetting that on the same ground they might practise polygamy. They practised it on the ground that it was not prohibited under the new dispensation; just as if every form of sin may be justified, which Jesus and his disciples did not specifically condemn, while they were introducing a system which strikes a blow at the radical principle of sinfulness. They practised it on the ground that it was for the benefit of the enslaved to take them from a condition of barbarism and place them in a civilized country; forgetting that wrong may be done to others in the attempt to benefit them. They practised it on the ground that if they did not, others would, enjoy the advantage of the traffic and the labor; just as if the wrong-doing of others can make an action right, which is inherently sinful.

Under the influence of deceptive considerations like these, the reflecting and the pious not only did not interfere with others, but they themselves encouraged the accursed traffic in human bones and sinews, and shared, it may be, in the unrighteous gains.

And thus the trade went on. All along the slave coast in Africa the native tribes felt a new stimulus to war in the hope of making captives in the open field, or in the defenceless villages. The man-hunter, like a staunch bloodhound, pursued his game along the streams, and among the palm groves: The mercenary mariner was waiting in the ship to purchase the captive negroes. And, the planter stood ready, on this side of the the ocean, to receive them and drive them to their unremitting toil. Many generations passed away, and still the same shrieks of terror were heard night and day all along the coast of Guinea. The same groans of despair went up from the slave-ship in the solitude of the Atlantic. The same agonies, mental and bodily, were vented forth in blood and tears under the lash or the reproaches of many an unfeeling owner or overseer.

This was done and suffered in God's world, beneath the open eye of heaven! Where then slept the thunder? Where was the red right-hand of Him who hath said, Vengeance is mine, I will repay? Behold a thousand years are in His sight as one day, and he that cometh, will come as the Judge of the whole earth, to render righteous retribution to the slave and his oppressor.

To the disgrace of our nation, the slave-trade was legalised more than twenty years after the formation of our Constitution; because, forsooth, two proud sisters in our national family, South Carolina and Georgia, would not otherwise adopt it. Yes, even in the very charter of our liberty, provision was made for imposing bondage upon others. It stands in these words, in strange discord with the general tone of the instrument—"The migration or importation of such persons, as any of the States, now existing, may choose to admit, shall not be prohibited by the Congress, prior to the year 1808; but a tax may be imposed on such importation not exceeding ten dollars." It would seem as if the general term, 'persons,' was substituted for the word *slaves*, to conceal the disgrace of the article.

Thus our nation, in its federal capacity, became involved in the guilt of the slave trade.

In consequence of this constitutional permission, the business was carried on upon a large scale. The fiends doubled their diligence, because their time was short.

By importation and by the natural increase, the number of slaves in the United States amounted, in 1810, two years after the prohibition of the trade, to 1,377,780; in 1820, 1,771,658; in 1830, to 2,330,039; and at the same rate, they must at the present amount to more than 2,600,000.

And now what is the *condition* of these 2,600,000 human beings?

In answering this question, it should be said, that there is a considerable variety in their condition, depending on the state of public sentiment in different communities, and upon the individual character of the master. Slavery puts on one form in Louisiana, and a milder form in Virginia; and hence the different and contradictory statements on this subject.

The people of the Northern States have thought too much of the physical, and too little of the moral and intellectual condition of the slaves. A New England man, with all his peculiar home comforts and conveniences about him, on his cultivated lands, which he holds in dependence upon no earthly superior, thinks of the slave as stinted in food, as half naked, as the tenant of some wretched cabin, built up with logs, with no floor but the hard earth; as toiling every day beyond his strength, and as utterly neglected in sickness and old age. He very likely gets his views of the whole subject from some high-wrought description of the physical sufferings which some individuals have endured, and which making a strong impression on his mind, are readily associated with the bare mention of slavery; so that the picture of slavery in his mind is a caricature in which the physical evils stand in the fore ground in strong relief, while the moral and intellectual evils are thrown far back into the shade. Now, independently of their healthy appearance, the single fact that they increase so rapidly is proof that the physical condition of the slaves, taking them in the mass, is not so wretched as it sometimes supposed to be. Indeed I have never known a New England man who had resided six months in one of the slave-holding States, who was not ready to say, that, in his early opinions, on this point, he had done great injustice to the South. Involuntary labor is comparatively unprofitable; so that slave-owners would in many cases find it impossible to furnish from that labor greater means of physical comfort to the slaves, without impoverishing themselves.

But for their moral and intellectual and legal condition generally, no apology can be made. Look at it:

I. No provision is made for their instruction in even the lowest branches of school education, or in the doctrines and duties of religion.

II. In some of the States, direct laws have been passed against their instruction. The prejudices of the whites are so strong on this subject, that in one instance, a gentleman who was determined to instruct his own slaves in a Sunday School, found it necessary to go armed to the school for his own protection.—Hodgson's Travels, p. 217.

III. If some of the better sort go through the ceremony of marriage, the law does not render it binding, since what God has joined together man may put asunder, by selling one of the parties, to be carried to a distant section of the country. The child too, after having lived to the age of five or six years in one of those miserable cabins, finds that a power comes in between him and his natural protectors. The parent looks upon the child as the property of another, which may be taken from him at any moment. The child looks upon the parent as the dependent upon another's will; and in despising him, learns to despise himself..

IV. They are not permitted to give testimony in a Court of Justice against the whites.

V. In most of the slave holding States, masters are forbidden to emancipate their slaves unless they remove them from the territory of the State.

VI. Slaves are, for the most part, considered as things rather than as persons, as machines, the moving power of which is fear, either of reproaches or the lash.

This, then, is the condition of 2,600,000 human beings in this boasted land of freedom, intelligence and virtue!

And what must be the influence of their condition on their character? Denied the means of instruction, they must be ignorant. Extensively not enjoying the ordinances of religion, extensively they must be heathen in a country denominated Christian, or else the subjects of a blind fanaticism. Not furnished by their masters with the comforts of life, they feel strongly the temptation to steal, especially as the property upon which they can lay their hands is the production of slave labor, and therefore viewed, in their loose notions of morality, as their own. Finding that it is just as well for them to consume as much and work as little as they can, they are lazy and wasteful. Their intellect not improved by exercise, their social feelings not refined by the charities of domestic life, and their sense of manhood crushed by oppression, they become stupid, or sullen, or sensual, or heedless, or vindictive, as the case may be. Not exercising the rights, and enjoying the privileges of freemen, they prove the truth of the maxim, that "the day which makes a man a slave, takes away half his worth." Indeed, by the Constitution, in the ratio of representation, the slave is viewed but as a fraction of a man.

I am now, in the II. branch of my discourse, to speak of the *history, condition* and *character*, of the FREE COLORED POPULATION in our country.

When the accursed traffic in human flesh was first engaged in by an Englishman, Queen Elizabeth said to him, "if the Africans were carried away without their own consent, it would be detestable, and would call down heaven's vengeance." This feeling of repugnance to slavery found a place in many hearts both in Great Britain, and in this country. And it showed itself extensively in the manumission of slaves, by individuals, before the States took up the subject. It showed itself in the reasonable complaints made by the Colonies against the Mother Country for encouraging the slave trade. In the original draft of the Declaration of Independence, very strong language was used on this subject, which was stricken out; not because it appeared to be too strong, but because it had "become so much hackneyed, that it seemed like mere truisms." The fact was, that while men were agitating the great subject of the rights of man, in connexion with their own liberty, which they were struggling to secure, they felt a strong sympathy with that unfortunate class of persons, who were loaded with still heavier chains. Indeed, it could hardly be possible, that while they were settling the fundamental principle that "all men are born free and equal, with certain unalienable rights, of which *liberty* is one," that they should not see that if this principle were acted on, it would emancipate the African.

Indeed this principle, whether true or false, was acted on by Massachusetts as early as the year 1780, and was introduced into her Bill of Rights for the very purpose of making it a basis for the abolition of slavery. It was acted on by Pennsylvania for the emancipation of her slaves in the same year, and even one day earlier than the former State. It was acted on successively by other States, who followed Pennsylvania and Massachusetts in the good work of proclaiming liberty to the slave, until now twelve of the twenty-four are virtually redeemed from the reproach and the curse of slavery.

While the process of emancipation has been going on, and the free colored population has been increasing up to 350,000, their present number, the inquiry arises, What is their present condition and character? Has liberty elevated the one and improved the other so much that the philanthropist may be encouraged to go on with the work of emancipation?

Now it must be confessed, that taken as a whole, they are in a degraded *condition*. Occasionally, individuals, by by great exertions, gain a good education, acquire property, and rise to a respectable standing: these however are only scattered instances, which are told of rather as matters of wonder.

The laws of the several States do not, for the most part, regard them as freemen, though they may call them so. "They take away the form, but leave them in the possession of the spirit of slavery." An attempt has been made to deny them the very name of citizen under the laws; while openly some of the most important privileges of citizenship have been denied to them.

Moreover, public sentiment holds them down in a bondage even more bitter than do the laws. It denies to them the privilege of being employed in most of the higher professions, and thus denies to them the liberalising, elevating influences, which these professions are found to exert upon their votaries. I do not mean that a negro cannot, if he chooses, study law; but what motive has he for studying it, when he sees that he must enter the profession with fearful odds against his success? I do not mean that a negro cannot apply his mind to politics; yet what community would be willing to elevate him to an important office, even if the law should permit it? In proof that public sentiment keeps them in a degraded condition, look at those occasions that have called forth an expression of public sentiment on this subject. Call to mind the opposition made to the establishment of a College for their especial benefit in one of the most respectable towns in New England. Call to mind the law subsequently passed in the State of Connecticut, intended to operate and actually operating against the instruction of the colored population. Call to mind the outrages committed at Canterbury, the mobs in New-York and other large towns, and the excitability of the public mind, in opposition to some who have attempted to raise them from their depression.

Besides all this, in some parts of the country they are kidnapped and sold into slavery. And even in the District of Columbia, to the disgrace of our nation be it said, a free citizen of one of the States, if his skin is colored, is liable to be seized and thrown into prison without even the imputation of a crime, and then sold into servitude for life to pay his jail fees!

Do not these and other things of a like character, prove as clearly as sunlight, that the free blacks are in a degraded, discouraging condition, and that they have but few motives comparatively for honorable enterprise and exertion?

And their *character*, especially that of the adult male part of the population, is generally as low as their condition. It is just what you would expect it to be, when you look at the circumstances of their situation. They are comparatively ignorant, as every one knows; addicted to vice, as proved by the records of the prison; poor and improvident, as proved by the annals of the alms-house.

Here, then, we have these 350,000 human beings, thus degraded in character and condition. And the question comes to us, with all its momentous importance, *What shall be done with them?* Shall they remain here, and become an integral part of the nation, and be admitted to all the rights and privileges of the whites; or shall they, and others who may become free, be colonized on the coast of Africa?

In answering this question, I propose in the III. branch

of my discourse, to speak of the *character* and *object* of the AMERICAN COLONIZATION SOCIETY.

This Society was formed in the winter of 1817, and the centre of its operations was very properly fixed at Washington. "The object to which its attention is to be exclusively directed, [I quote the second Article of the Constitution] is to promote and execute a plan for colonizing, with their consent, the free people of color residing in our country, in Africa, or such other place as Congress shall deem most expedient. And the Society shall act, to effect this object, in co-operation with the General Government, and such of the States as may adopt regulations on the subject."

Here the object is distinctly stated, namely, to promote and execute a plan for colonizing, with their consent, the free people of color residing in our country. There can then be no mistake on this point. This object, when it became understood, commended itself to some of the wisest, and best, and most influential men of the nation. Undoubtedly some patronized it from good, and some from bad motives; some, because they thought they could see in it the sure, but effectual means for ridding the country of slavery; and others, because they thought that by ridding the slave holding States of the free blacks, it would render slaves more valuable.

It was, at the time this Society was formed, supposed that the free people of color generally would be pleased to emigrate to Africa, as their father-land; that, escaping from the disabilities under which they labored here, they would successfully emulate the whites in their devotion to learning, civil polity, and the arts; that the Colony, patronized by the General Government, would help to destroy the traffic in slaves, which was still carried on upon the coast; and that it would exert a salutary influence upon Africa by the introduction of civilization and christianity into those barbarous regions.

Proceeding judiciously in their addresses to the public, though some mistakes were probably made in the management of their affairs, they succeeded in a good degree in removing jealousies which arose both at the north and the south. "Fourteen of the States have already united with the plan;" and men of every religious denomination, and of every political party, from every section of the country, have lent their influence and their means to promote its operations.

It has however been assailed, in no measured terms, as unworthy of our confidence and support.

One charge brought against it is, that it speaks one language to the northern abolitionist, and another to the southern slave-holder; and thus 'incurs the guilt of duplicity. Now, in reply, I would only say, that the agents and friends of the Society may have been injudicious in their statements; but this should not involve the Society in guilt, unless it has by some act made itself responsible for what has been said by indiscreet friends. Besides, in some respects, it is proper to hold different language to different individuals; inasmuch as the minds of men are different; and the arguments, if they are adapted to different minds, will of course be different. Paul used very different arguments in addressing the Athenian heathen on Mars Hill, from what he did when he addressed the men of Israel at Antioch, though his object was the same in both instances, namely, to make them christians.

Another charge brought against the Society is, that the Colony has not flourished as much as it was expected it would, and that therefore there is either bad management on the part of its officers, or else they are engaged in an undertaking that is hopeless from the inherent difficulties in the case. Now, that there should be some bad management, was to be expected; and that there should be great difficulties in such a novel undertaking, was likewise to be expected: Still, however the Colony, with all the bad management, and all the inherent difficulties in the case, with all the sickness which has scourged it at different times, has, as you well know, flourished more than did either the Colony of the Puritans at Plymouth, or that of the Cavaliers on James River.

That a trading Colony, like this, should be able to exert

a very salutary influence upon Africa that shall be extensive immediately, is hardly to be expected. Moral causes are frequently slow in their operation. The people of Africa are made up of three distinct races, viz: the Moors, who, under one name and another, occupy the north; the Caffres, who inhabit the eastern part; and the Negroes, who dwell in the middle and western portions. Beside these, there are some tribes of a characte quite peculiar, as for instance the Hottentots. The languages of Africa must, according to Seetzen, amount to one hundred or one hundred and fifty. To effect the civilization of any considerable portion of that quarter of the globe, must of course be the work of time; but it is a work of such vast consequence, that every attempt that promises to accomplish even a small part of it, ought to be made. Let every man who values the religion of Jesus Christ, rejoice then, that the standard of the cross has been planted on the shores of Africa; and that though some strong arms that bore it there, and some true hearts that beat high in the hope that multitudes would gather around it, are now buried dust, still other hearts as warm and other arms as strong are there to labor and pray for the good of Africa.

Another charge brought against the Society is, that it is inadequate to the purpose of preventing the slave trade. Now I am ready to allow, that while the pirates stand ready to receive slaves, and pay for them on the coast of Africa, and multitudes not only in South America but in some parts of the United States are ready to purchase them of the pirates, it will be difficult entirely to break up this detestable traffic. But it has already done much, and promises to accomplish more. It has been stated on good authority, that twelve years ago, 5000 slaves were annually carried from what is now the territory of the Colony. Now for 100 miles along the coast, not a slaver dare unfold his canvass. This surely is something. Besides, it furnishes an asylum for the slaves that are captured from the pirates. "It has already procured the emancipation of about 3000 slaves." This surely is something. It cannot, indeed, for a long time to come, do all that ought to be done; but it can do enough to furnish a strong claim to our patronage.

Another charge against the Society is, that some of its friends have applied the doctrines of expediency, as the rule of right, to this subject to such an extent, that it quiets the conscience of the slave-holder, in regard to the sin of slavery. I have sometimes been disposed to believe, that at least, some of the friends of this Society have thought too much of consequences, and too little of the fixed and eternal principles of right. Indeed, I have sometimes been astonished that good men could say so much about slavery, and yet exhibit so little abhorrence of the practice; and that some of them should, in their conversation, and in their writings, labor, in effect, to shew that the slave has no very good claim to liberty, as a right; and that the slave-holders generally, incur little or no guilt in holding the blacks in bondage; that they are to be pitied rather than blamed. Still however, the Society, as such, should not be held responsible for the mistakes of its friends.

Another charge against the Society is, that it is doing nothing directly to promote the abolition of slavery. On this point I have only to say, that inasmuch as its constitution declares that the object to which it shall be exclusively directed, is the colonization of the free people of color, with their own consent, residing in our country, it could not consistently or honorably devote itself to another object, namely, the emancipation of the slaves. This it must leave to other agents. But do you ask, Why was the Society limited in its action to this particular object? For the plain reason that this object is large enough to call forth all the energies of the Association, and likewise for the reason that it was an object upon which the north and the south could unite in harmonious action. Let then the Colonization Society confine itself to the object to which it is pledged, and let the Antislavery Society promote, by judicious means, the abolition of slavery.

We come now to the IV. branch of my discourse, in which I propose to speak of the *character* and *object* of the ANTISLAVERY SOCIETY.

This Society was formed in December, 1833. The second and third articles state what are the objects for which it was established:

"Article 2.—The objects of this Society are the entire abolition of slavery in the United States. While it admits that each State in which slavery exists, has, by the Constitution of the United States, the exclusive right to legislate in regard to its abolition, it shall aim to convince all our fellow-citizens, by arguments addressed to their understanding and consciences, that slave-holding is a heinous sin in the sight of God, and that the duty, safety, and best interests of all concerned require its immediate abandonment without expatriation. The Society will also endeavor, in a constitutional way, to influence Congress to put an end to the domestic slave-trade, and to abolish slavery in all those portions of the country which come under its control, especially in the District of Columbia; and likewise to prevent the extension of it to any State, that may be hereafter admitted into the Union."

"Article 3.—This Society shall aim to elevate the character and condition of the people of color by encouraging their intellectual, moral and religious improvement, and by removing public prejudice, that thus they may, according to their intellectual and moral worth, share an equality with the whites of civil and religious privileges; but this Society will never in any way countenance the oppressed in vindicating their rights by an appeal to physical force."

We see here what are the objects for which this Society was established; and do they not, in the main, commendably commend themselves to the mind as important objects? Its aim is to abolish slavery; and what is slavery? Let a southern man answer.

"It is that condition enforced by the laws of one half of this Confederacy, in which one portion of the community, called Masters, is allowed such power over another portion called Slaves, as

1, To deprive them of the entire earnings of their own, except only so much as is necessary to continue labor itself by continuing healthful existence; thus committing clear robbery;

2, To reduce them to the necessity of universal concubinage by denying them the civil rights of marriage; thus breaking up the dearest relations of life, and encouraging universal prostitution;

3, To deprive them of the means and opportunities of moral and intellectual culture, and many States making it a high penal offence to teach them to read; thus perpetuating whatever evil there is that proceeds from ignorance;

4, To set up between parents and their children an authority higher than the impulse of nature and the laws of God; which breaks up the authority of the father over his own offspring, and at pleasure separates the mother to a returnless distance from her child; thus abrogating the clearest laws of nature; thus outraging all decency and justice, and degrading and oppressing thousands upon thousands of beings created in the image of the Most High God. This is slavery as it is daily exhibited in every slave State. This is that 'dreadful but unavoidable necessity' for which you may hear so many thousands uttering excuses in all parts of the land." Listen to another witness:

"Its effects upon those who maintain it, and in some measure upon those who witness it and consent to it, are indolence, diabolical passions, deadness to the claims of justice and the calls of mercy, a worldly spirit, and contempt for a large portion of our fellow creatures." This is the language of one who, from his boyhood, was a slave holder.

Look then at the magnitude of the evil to be removed, and the immense work of removing it, and then tell me whether in the division of labor for the accomplishment of good, in the various moral enterprises of the day, this object is not large enough to demand a separate and independent voluntary association for the purpose. I am sure that the American Antislavery Society will find enough to do without interfering with the benevolent object for which the American Colonization Society was established. Let it go on then to enlighten the public mind as to the nature, the guilt and the danger of slavery: Let it endeavor in a constitutional way to influence Congress to put an end to the *domestic slave trade* and to *abolish slavery in all those portions of our common country that come under its control;* especially in the District of Columbia. Let it endeavor to elevate the character and condition of the people of color, by encouraging their intellectual, moral and religious improvement.

But it is said that this Society contemplates political action. If however this action is in accordance with the provisions of the Constitution of these United States, just as the Colonization Society contemplates political action, what fault can be found with it on this score?

But it is said that this Society excites the slaves to resist the laws. This is directly contrary to its constitution, which declares that this Society will never in any way countenance the oppressed in vindicating their rights by an appeal to force.

Many charges have been brought against the friends of this Society, some of which are very possibly true. I do not stand here to defend every sentiment contained in the constitution of the Society, any more than I would defend every sentiment in the Constitution which is the great charter of our liberties. Much less would I defend every thing that has been said and done by the friends of this Society. What they have said, may sometimes have been imprudent; what they have done, may have been injudicious. May they learn wisdom from any mistakes they may have committed. Still however, are not the objects, in the main, at which they aim, most important objects? Shall nothing be done in this age of benevolent action to break the fetters of the slave? Shall the disgrace and the guilt of holding human beings in bondage, and putting out the eyes of their mind, and debasing their immortal nature, always rest upon this land of freemen? Shall the cry of millions constantly arise to the ears of Him who redeemed Israel, and must we stop our ears? Shall we harden our hearts?

No! Slavery cannot forever exist on this soil, won by the blood of freemen from the strong arm of the oppressor.

Slavery is *disgraceful*, and national honor requires its abolition. Slavery is *unprofitable*, and national prosperity requires its abolition. Slavery is *sinful*, and national duty requires its abolition. Slavery is *dangerous*, and the threatened judgments of heaven require its abolition. We followed England in putting an end to the slave trade, and as sure as there is any efficacy in moral causes, we shall follow her in the abolition of slavery. The late glorious act by which she gave freedom to eight hundred thousand slaves in her Colonies, speaks to our country in a language which is distinct and persuasive. The trumpet-voice of liberty comes to us from that side of the ocean, in loud and stirring tones; and is answered on this, by the exulting shouts of millions! As it sounds through the land, champions in the cause of freedom will arise here, as there, to contend earnestly and successfully for the oppressed and degraded slave, until, in the language of the prophet, they "loose the bands of wickedness, and undo the heavy burdens, and let the oppressed go free, and break every yoke."

In the rapid view which I have taken of the subject before us, I have been able only to glance at the several topics, instead of bestowing upon them that longer and closer examination which they would demand, if they were not familiar to your minds. Enough I trust, however, has been said, to show to the candid and intelligent, that the Societies ought not to appear in hostile array against each other; THAT EACH DOES, IN THE MAIN, ACT IN THE NAME AND BY THE AUTHORITY OF JESUS, AND THEREFORE SHOULD NOT BE FORBIDDEN.

Here then we have two classes of human beings who cry to us for help, and He who made of one blood all the nations of men to dwell on all the face of the earth, will not allow us to close our ears to their cry. The Colonization Society have benevolently undertaken to promote the welfare of the one class, by opening for them an asylum in the land of their fathers. The Antislavery Society have benevolently undertaken to promote the welfare of the other, by laboring to accomplish their emancipation. The objects thus aimed at are so distinct, that they require each of them a distinct and independent organization for their accomplishment. Each of them are necessarily attended with many difficulties; and why increase these difficulties by controversy? The Colonization Society has enough to do, in taking care of the Colony established in Liberia. The Antislavery Society has enough to do, in promoting the abolition of slavery in the United States.

But it is asked, Why may not the two Societies be amalgamated, and thus form one powerful association, embodying in itself the intelligence, the wealth, the benevolence, and the piety of the land? This very plainly is impossible, since the objects at which they aim are different. But is not this difference merely apparent? Do they not both aim at the welfare of the colored population? This is to confound the motive, with the immediate and professed object. But will not the efforts of the Colonization Society eventuate in the emancipation of the slaves, the consummation so devoutly wished by the Antislavery Society? Perhaps so; but this desirable event, which may possibly be promoted by the indirect and the accidental agency of the *one*, will probably be accomplished by the direct influence of the *other*. These two Societies, in their endeavors to promote the welfare of the blacks, are laboring in contiguous Provinces, and therefore can conveniently aid each other. If the Antislavery Society shall succeed in promoting the emancipation of the slaves, then it will assist the Colonization Society, by furnishing it with an opportunity for a better selection of emigrants for building up the Colony. On the other hand, the greater the number the Colonization Society transports to Liberia, the more room there will be for future and progressive emancipation, without endangering the peace and safety of the country. In this way they can be helpers of each other, as they ought to be, while they are efficiently promoting the several objects for which they were established. Why then should these Societies, thus capable of benefitting each other, weaken their energies and waste their resources, in attacking each other, and in the consequently necessary self-defence? Why should these contests continue to produce among some of the partisans of each, a frenzied excitement, resulting in denunciation and outrages upon decorum and propriety; or in riots, and in outrages upon the laws of the land and the safety of individuals. Let us aid each of these associations as best we can. But let each confine itself to its legitimate object. Let not the friends of the one, in this land where the freedom of speech and of the press is guarantied to us by the Constitution, attempt to stifle discussion. Our country has already been sufficiently disgraced. Let not the friends of the other, discuss the subject in the angry tones of denunciation, lest in this way they ruin a good cause. Let not Ephraim envy Judah, or Judah vex Ephraim. Let each remember what Jesus said to his disciples, "FORBID THEM NOT." LET EACH CONTINUE TO CAST OUT DEVILS IN THE NAME OF CHRIST, THOUGH IT FOLLOWS NOT THE OTHER.

Friends and patrons of the Colonization Society: we come this night to ask you to continue your friendship; and to prove your friendship by substantial patronage. Look for a moment towards Africa, and see the degraded and wretched population of that land of the sun. Think of the crimes committed there, the blood shed there, the tears that flow there, and that night of intellectual and moral darkness which reigns there; and then ask yourself, whether as an American, whether as a philanthropist, whether as a christian, you owe nothing to Africa? We have looked with a parent's feelings towards that Colony. When it has flourished, we have rejoiced: when it has been in affliction, we have felt as did Granville Sharpe, when he wrote in 1787, "I have had but melancholy accounts of my poor little ill-thriven, swarthy daughter, the unfortunate Colony of Sierra Leone." But his Colony afterwards flourished and so will ours, if we do a parent's duty to ours, as he did to his. Let not then that bright vision of the future, which shows to us, like the Mirage of the desart, villages, cultivated farms, and green fields, in that waste region, vanish like the Mirage, leaving us, as it does the traveler, to a cruel disappointment. Rather let it prove, in that moral desart, like an Oasis in the great Sahara, upon which the soul wearied, in search of good there, may love to repose. Let the Colony, whatever may be its influence upon our own country, still be the "Star of Hope" to Africa. Let it stand like her own Pharos, in the night of ages which rests upon that stormy coast. Through its influence, let the art of agriculture be taught to the lazy, to the improvident, to the cannibal tribes. Let Africa thus become, as in former times, the granary of the world. Let her, as a Queen, put on her ancient crown of wheat ears. Above all, let her tears be dried, her wounds healed, her soul washed, and purified in the blood of Christ, and clothed in the graces of the gospel. Instead of temples in honor of deceased monarchs, built with clay mixed with human blood, let there be temples consecrated to the Prince of Peace. Instead of the Poorrah, the black tribunal, which "sends death," it may be without a hearing, let trial by jury be introduced. Let the giddy dance, which through the whole night, is animated by the hoarse sounds of the ivory trumpet, give place to the quiet enjoyments of christian life, to the decencies of christian worship, to the animating, elevating hymn of christian thanksgiving.

Do you ask, *What* shall I do? Give this Society your influence; give it your prayers, give it your money. Your influence is needed, to encourage its friends; your prayers are needed, to bring down upon it the blessing of heaven; your money is needed, because the Society, without means, can accomplish nothing. Gird yourself up this night to the high purpose of making some sacrifice, to lay the foundation of a great christian nation on the coast of Africa. I ask this sacrifice for a noble object. I ask it of you in the name of my country, stained as she is with guilt. I ask it in the name of Africa, deeply injured and suffering Africa. I ask it in the name of Him, who was rich and became poor for our sakes.

NOTES.

Note A.

As the public mind is already sufficiently excited on the subject of slavery, I have endeavored, throughout the foregoing discourse, to present the subject, in a calm and dispassionate way, for considerate action. So far as I am informed, there has never been a period when men were so ready to speak, to write, and to act on the general subjects connected with the condition of the colored population of our country. Look at the newspaper discussions, the anniversary speeches, and the reports of various associations; the able investigations presented in the most respectable periodicals; and at the arguments and facts spread before the reading and thinking public, in the African Repository and the Antislavery Reporter; and you will be convinced that public feeling is strongly excited. One party says to the other, You are seeking to dissolve the Union, by raising up jealousies in the south; you are exciting slaves to rebellion; you are trying to promote intermarriages between the blacks and the whites.—The other in reply says, You sacrifice your conscience to your fears; you are guilty of hypocrisy in your professions of regard for the welfare of the blacks, inasmuch as you are endeavoring to banish them from this land of their birth. Thus there is crimination and recrimination. Now the two-fold danger in this state of things is, that the friends of the one Society shall, in their endeavors to produce an abhorrence of the sin of slavery, bring indiscriminate charges against slave-holders, and thus calumniate many good men among them; and moreover, that the friends of the other Society, in their desire to conciliate the south, and to defend good men who are slave-holders, against the calumnious charges brought against them, shall become the apologists of slavery.

Note B.

In opposition to the Colonization Society, it has been said, that it is evidently absurd to suppose that the vast number of slaves in our country, even if they should be inclined to emigrate to Liberia, could be transported thither. Take a single fact: By official statements, it appears that the number of emigrants who arrived at Quebec in ten years, from 1825 to 1834, was 1,192,258. The colonization of all the colored people in the United States, if they are inclined to it, is practicable, provided individual enterprise is aided by the General and the State Governments. Whether the blacks will universally, or even generally incline to the measure, is another question. Indeed, from personal conversation with a considerable number of the slaves, at the time the Society was formed, and likewise at a later period, I am convinced that the opposition of the blacks to the scheme of African Colonization lies too deep in their hearts to be easily eradicated. Time seems to have strengthened this opposition. They seem to say to the whites, You first injured our fathers by forcing them away from all they held dear in their native country, Africa; and now, you would urge us away from all we hold dear in our native country, America. The injury is the same in both cases. You pretend, indeed, that it is for our benefit that we are to be sent to Africa: so your fathers pretended that it was for the benefit of our fathers, that they should be brought to America. This is our home. Here we wish to live. Some of them have strong local attachments. A friend of mine, in Virginia, soon after he became pious, called his slaves together, about a hundred in number, and said to them, "I am willing to give all of you your freedom, and carry you to Ohio; and furnish you with a year's provision. You need not tell me now, whether you will accept of my offer: Wait until next Monday, when I will meet you again to receive your answer." The week that followed this conversation, was a melancholy week on that plantation. When Monday arrived, they all assembled to say to him, that they loved their present home too well to wish for any change. They wept, and cried, "Do keep us, Master; don't send us away."

But while I see but little reason to believe that the blacks will generally be disposed, without coercive measures, to go to Africa, I have no doubt that a very considerable number of well-qualified emigrants can be obtained—enough indeed, in due time, to stud the whole western coast with settlements; especially if proper measures are adopted for promoting the cause of education among them.

Note C.

From the last Report of the American Colonization Society, it appears "that the whole number of emigrants, including the expedition of last year, and the recaptured Africans, (a part of whom only were removed to this country) has been 3,123, while the present population of the Colony is stated to be 2,816. About 50 of the colonists are believed to have been absent in the country when this census was taken." In regard to the sickness which has diminished the Colony, the managers, in the same report, make the following encouraging remarks:

"The history of Colonization in America, proves how impotent were events, in themselves most afflictive and disheartening, to arrest the progress of settlements founded by men who grew wise in adversity, and gathered resolution and strength from defeat. The genius of our nation, sprung from the Colonies of Plymouth and Jamestown, rebukes the despondency which would augur destruction to Liberia, because dark clouds have hung over it, and many valuable lives perished in laying its foundations. Nearly one half the first Plymouth emigrants died in the course of four months. The first three attempts to plant a Colony in Virginia totally failed. In six months, ninety of the one hundred settlers, who first landed at Jamestown, died. Subsequently in the same brief period, the inhabitants of this Colony were reduced from five hundred to sixty; and long after, when £150,000 had been expended on that Colony, and nine thousand people had been sent thither, its population amounted to but 1800 souls. It is the opinion of Dr. Mechlin, that the settlement just commenced at Grand Bassa, is more favorable to health than Monrovia; and that future emigrants should be first sent to that place."

"The cause of education is making progress; nearly all the settlers wish their children to enjoy its advantages, and the common schools, six in number, (three of them sustained by a benevolent society of ladies in Philadelphia) are well conducted and attended. The Auxiliary Colonization Society of Massachusetts, appropriated early in the year, $1,000 towards the establishment and support of a school, with two teachers, to be called the Massachusetts Colonial Free School. Ample and judicious regulations have been drawn up by that Society, for the management of this school, which is to be under the immediate control of a committee consisting of the Colonial Agent or the Mayor of Monrovia, and two other persons, to be annually elected by the citizens of the Colony; and it is expected soon to be in operation. The Managers are pleased to learn that Mr. A. H. Savage, who has entered upon a course of benevolent action in the Colony, designs to commence a manual labor school at Millsburg; and his estimable character and practical knowledge, give reason to conclude, that it will be so conducted as to prove of large and extensive utility. Many of the ladies of New-York, of different denominations, have united to form a Society for the promotion of education in Liberia. It is proposed, by forming associations in the different churches, to raise in each church a sum adequate to the support of a single teacher. Several teachers have already offered their services, and the means for the support of some of them, are already pledged. The scheme excites much interest, and it is hoped that many churches will engage in this work of benevolence and mercy."

"The Managers can add little to the statements in their last report, in regard to the moral and religious interests of the Colony. The number of churches or meeting-houses in the various settlements, is nine; the Sabbath and public worship are well observed; many of the recaptured Africans have united themselves to the church; and the christian community have manifested a desire to impart religious knowledge to the African tribes. In May last, the Board of Missions of the Baptist Church in Monrovia, appointed Adam W. Anderson a Missionary for one year, among Vye people at Cape Mount, and instructed him not only to preach the gospel to the adults of this tribe, but to teach the English language to their children. All the native Africans in the neighborhood of the Colony, are prepared to receive instruction in letters, the arts and christianity; and many of the chiefs have offered to make grants of land, on the simple condition, that their youth shall enjoy the advantages of an English education. Thousands of human beings, debased in intellect and darkly bound in vice, invoke the spirit of missionary enterprise to extend its triumphs over an almost unlimited field; and in their characters renovated, and lives purified by its influence, to find for every labor and sacrifice, an ample and durable reward"

Note D.

Since writing the discourse, I have read the letter of Capt Voorhees to the Secretary of the Navy, dated Dec, 14, 1833. In it he says, "It is reported that a number of vessels for Cuba are now on this coast, employed in the odious traffic of the slave-trade: a steam-boat is highly necessary here, as a *guarda costa*, and to examine into the matter." There is great reason to apprehend, that as long as slavery exists on this side of the ocean, there always will be found those who will bring the African seller and the American buyer together, even at the hazard of suffering the punishment of piracy. Edwards, in his History of the West Indies, says, "Whether it be possible for any nation in Europe, singly considered, to prevent its subjects from procuring slaves from Africa, so long as Africa shall continue to sell, is a point on which I have many doubts; but *none* concerning the conveying the slaves so purchased into every Island in the West Indies, in spite of the *maritime force of all Europe*. No man who is acquainted with the extent of the uninhabited coast of the larger of these Islands, the facility of landing in every part of them, the prevailing winds, and the numerous creeks and harbors, * * * * can hesitate a moment to pronounce that an attempt to prevent the introduction of slaves into our West India Colonies, would be like that of chaining the winds, or giving laws to the ocean." What he declares to be true on this subject, in regard to the West Indies, is likewise true in regard to this country, and substantially for the same reasons. Indeed, some parts of the Southern States afford still greater facilities for smuggling slaves into them, than do the West Indies. What then is the effectual remedy for this contraband slave-trade? The abolition of slavery: Destroy the market, and the trade ceases.

Note B.

To show the evils of the slave-trade in its influence upon Africa, I will add some extracts from the 9th No. of Malte-Brun's Universal Geography:

"One of these native merchants, known by the name of Ben Johnson, had carried off a free young woman, and sold her to an English Captain. As he returned with the reward of his villainy, other negroes, dispatchpatched by the prince or the chiefs of the village, attacked him, bound him, and crying, 'off with the thief,' took him to the vessel, and offered him for sale. It was in vain that Ben Johnson appealed to the friendship of the European negro-dealer, reminding him that he was a free man, and his most active hand in procuring slaves. 'No matter,' says the unfeeling Englishman, 'since the people sell you, I purchase you;' and instantly fixed his fetters. In other instances, a horrible avarice dissolves all the ties of kindred. Mothers are seen selling their children at an early age, for a few bushels of rice. One day, a stout young African took his little son to sell him to the Europeans; the latter, more cunning, and better acquainted with the language of the foreigners, showed them that a man of the strength and size of his father, was of more value than he, and thus prevailed with them to take him in his stead, though the latter kept calling out, that 'no son had a right to sell his father.'

"It cannot be denied, that these and other enormities are purely the offspring of the infamous traffic in negroes. The most dreadful thing is, that the African princes, in order to get possession of a hundred men, often sacrifice a thousand; for, when these despots do not find individuals whom they can condemn to be sold, they regularly hunt down the inhabitants of an entire village, like a flock of deer; some make an armed resistance, others fly to the woods, to the dens of lions and panthers, scarcely so merciless as their own compatriots. Several tracts of country have been depopulated by these atrocities.

"It is certain that the slaves are carried off against their will, and most frequently in all the agonies of the most poignant affliction. This is not denied: but it is said that they consist of captives who would otherwise be slain, or criminals condemned by courts of justice. The answer to this is, and it is proved beyond all possibility of contradiction, that wars are now undertaken, incessantly, for the express purpose of procuring slaves for the market; and that since the establishment of this traffic, every crime is punished by selling the offender to a dealer; accusations of witchcraft or adultery are always at hand to insure a supply to the traders on the coast; and if these fail, it is admitted, that by advancing a little brandy or gunpowder to the natives, a whole village may be legally carried off in satisfaction of the debt.

"The necessity of crowding on board of one vessel several hundred slaves, often produces the most horrible scenes. Attacked by pestilential fevers, by famine and death, the slave-ship becomes at once an hospital, a prison, and a school of inhumanity and crime. More than one half of the blacks that form the cargo kill themselves or die of disease; sometimes the Captain, reduced to a want of provisions, throws them alive into the sea to save the lives of the Europeans. The mariners employed in such a trade acquire a ferocious character, and afterwards stain the soil of Europe with crimes worthy only of degraded Africa.

"The following extract from the Bibliotheque Ophthalmique, will give some idea of the horrors of what is called the middle passage:— 'The Rodeur sailed from Havre on the 24th of January, 1819, for the coast of Africa, to purchase slaves. When under the line, it was perceived that the negroes, who were heaped together in the hold, and between decks, had contracted a considerable inflammation in the eyes. They were successively brought on deck, in order that they might breathe a purer air. But it was necessary to discontinue this practice, because they threw themselves into the sea, locked in each other's arms. On the arrival of the ship at Guadaloupe, the crew was in a most deplorable condition. Of the negroes, *thirty-nine had become blind, and were thrown overboard.*'"

Note F.

There is an apathy on the subject of the existence of slavery in the District of Columbia, placed as it is, under the control of Congress, that is absolutely alarming. There is a squeamishness about meddling with its abolition on the part of those who profess to abhor slavery, that is strongly in contrast with the robust virtue lately evinced in Great Britain, in breaking the chains of West India slavery. Say to these professed friends of liberty, Can we do nothing to destroy slavery in the south? Oh! we must not touch that subject; Congress must not touch that subject, placed as it is by the Constitution entirely under the control of the States. We must, as good citizens, submit to the constitutional laws of the land. Then say to them, You are in favor then of confining Congress to the exercise of those powers which are granted by the Constitution. Very well. And now as Congress, by the Constitution, has the sole right to legislate on subjects of slavery, let it go on to put an end to slavery then, and the disgraceful domestic slave trade, which is carried on there, every winter, in presence of the great Council of our Nation. Oh, no! we must not create jealousies in the south, by touching slavery in the District of Columbia. I do not attribute this view of the case to Mr. Gurley, the excellent Secretary of the American Colonization Society: I have known him too long, and respect him too much, and love him too well.

Now I must think, from considerable intercourse with southern gentlemen, that this view of the subject does great injustice to the south. There are men there who abhor slavery, and who would join heart and hand in ridding the whole land of slavery, even at the expense of great personal sacrifices. They mourn over the national sin and the national disgrace of slavery, and they would exult in making some national expiation for that sin by the abolition of slavery in the District of Columbia. Now the hands of this class of southern men are weakened, and their hearts discouraged, by the timid, time-serving policy that refuses to touch the subject of slavery and the slave-trade in the District of Columbia.

Look at some of the facts presented by Mr. Miner, in the preamble to the resolutions offered by him in the House of Representatives, January 9th, 1829:

"Whereas the laws in respect to slavery within the District have been almost entirely neglected; from which neglect, for nearly thirty years, have grown numerous and gross corruptions;

"Slave-dealers, gaining confidence from impunity, have made the seat of federal government their head-quarters for carrying on the domestic slave-trade;

"The public prisons have been extensively used, (perverted from the purposes for which they were erected,) for carrying on the domestic slave-trade;

"Officers of the federal government have been employed, and derive emoluments from carrying on the domestic slave-trade;

"Private and secret prisons exist in the District, for carrying on the traffic in human beings;

"The trade is not confined to those who are slaves for life, but persons having a limited time to serve, are bought by the slave-dealers, and sent where redress is hopeless;

"Others are kidnapped and hurried away before they can be rescued;

"Instances of death, from the anguish of despair, exhibited in the District, mark the cruelty of this traffic;

"Instances of maiming and suicide, executed or attempted, have been exhibited, growing out of this traffic within the District;

"Free persons of color coming into the District, are liable to arrest, imprisonment, and sale into slavery for life, for jail fees, if unable, from ignorance, misfortune, or fraud, to prove their freedom;

"Advertisements beginning, 'We will give cash for one hundred likely young negroes of both sexes, from eight to twenty-five years old,' contained in the public prints of the city, under the notice of Congress, indicate the openness and extent of the traffic;

"Scenes of human beings exposed at public vendue are exhibited here, permitted by the laws of the General Government;

"A grand jury of the District has presented the slave-trade as a grievance;

"A writer in a public print in the District has set forth 'that to those who have never seen a spectacle of the kind (exhibited by the slave trade) no description can give an adequate idea of its horrors;'

"To such an extent had this trade been carried in 1816, that a member of Congress from Virginia introduced a resolution in the House, 'That a committee be appointed to inquire into the existence of an *inhuman* and *illegal* traffic in slaves carried on in and through the District of Columbia, and report whether any, and what measures are necessary for putting a stop to the same.'

"The House of Representatives of Pennsylvania, at their last session, by an almost unanimous vote, expressed the opinion, 'that slavery within the District of Columbia ought to be abolished.'"

On this subject, a writer in the American Quarterly Review for September, 1833, remarks—

"Scarcely an evil attends the African slave-trade, which does not find its parallel in that carried on at the seat of government of the United States, by the license of the American people. The victims of the African slave-trade are taken by force, against their will; they are carried to a foreign country; they are torn from their friends, their wives, their children; they are chained; some of them were born free, and have been kidnapped by force or fraud. In which of these particulars is the Columbian slave-trade less atrocious? The black taken from the District, goes reluctantly; he is forced from the home of his love, to the unhealthy borders of the Mississippi; as much removed from the hope of revisiting it as if he was going to another continent; he is torn by violence, amid shrieks, and tears, and groans, and muttered imprecations, from the embraces of his wife and children; he goes handcuffed and chained; he was born free, and was stolen from Delaware or Maryland. Ought not such a traffic to be abolished, 'absolutely, totally, and immediately?'

"It may perhaps excite surprise that this traffic has not long since been abolished. The great reason that this result has not taken place, undoubtedly is, that the public generally are not at all aware of the nature and extent of the evil. All that may now be necessary, in order to put an end to the system, is to make the body of the people understand it. If this were done, a single session of Congress would not perhaps be suffered to pass before a reform was commenced."

The same writer still further remarks—

"It may perhaps be not amiss to say a few words as to the means by which the power of the national government may be called into action to suppress slavery in the District of Columbia. It should be recollected that Congress is never in advance of, but usually behind public opinion. It follows slowly but surely in the path taken by the people. The legislation of Congress is but the echo of the people's voice. If the people really desire slavery to be abolished at the seat of government, Congress will pass the statutes necessary to carry the object into effect. But it is in vain to expect the national legislature to adopt an important measure of this kind, which is sure to offend the prejudices of a large body in the community, unless the members feel confident that they are acting in conformity with the wishes of their constituents. A loud and decided expression of public sentiment is necessary to stimulate the sluggish force of Congress, and to overcome the *vis inertiæ* with which an established evil resists every attempt to remove it.

"The modes of acting upon Congress are so obvious and familiar, that it is needless to enlarge upon them. Those who are desirous of abolishing slavery in the District, must unite themselves together, and use the common means for diffusing information upon the subject throughout the country. Newspapers and other periodical journals and tracts can be made to exert a widely extended influence. Public meetings should be held, and as many petitions as possible sent to Congress, praying for the desired object. An expression of opinion on the subject might probably, by active exertions, be obtained from some of the state legislatures.

"It is not very difficult to rouse the nation, or rather the non-slave holding part of it, to powerful action, in order to remove the pollution of slavery from the seat of our government. The principles of the people on this subject are sound, and their feelings warm. To induce them to act, nothing more is necessary, as we have already intimated, than to make them familiar with the facts of the case. Let this be done, and the abolition of slavery in the District will be so easily effected, that men will hereafter wonder that it should have been endured there so long."

Note G.

But the grand objection to emancipation is, that the slaves are not qualified for freedom. Evidently there is considerable force in it. Could I see those who urge this objection actually doing any thing to insure their future qualification, I should feel that they have a right to urge it. Those who are opposed to the establishment of schools and seminaries of learning of a higher character, for the especial benefit of the colored youth of our country, had better be silent on this point. The truth seems to be, that slavery exerts a benumbing influence upon the unhappy subjects of it, to such a degree, that every one almost who has formed his character under its influence, becomes comparatively degraded in intellect, and in all the higher attributes of manhood, and unfit for the full enjoyment of liberty. Mr. Fox, while the subject of the abolition of the slave-trade was under consideration in the British Parliament, remarked with great truth, "that it might be as dangerous to liberate a man used to slavery, as in the case of one who had never seen day-light, to expose him at once to the meridian sun." While there is truth in the statement, that the slaves of the Southern States, as they now are, are not qualified for the exercise of some of the rights of freemen, still they might enjoy other of these rights without injury to themselves or others. Why might not the recent recommendation of the Synod of Kentucky, be universally followed, and all slaves born hereafter, be emancipated?

"The following declaration and resolutions (says the N. Y. Observer) were adopted by the Synod of Kentucky, at their meeting in Danville, Ky., last month, by a vote of 56 to 8.

"This Synod, believing that the system of absolute and hereditary domestic slavery, as it exists among the members of our communion, is repugnant to the principles of our holy religion as revealed in the sacred Scriptures, and that the continuance of the system any longer than is necessary to prepare for its safe and beneficial termination, is sinful, feel it their duty earnestly to recommend to all Presbyteries, Church Sessions, and people under their care, to commence immediate preparation for the termination of slavery among us; so that this evil may cease to exist with the present generation, and the future offspring of our slaves may be free.

"In recommending that emancipation be unanimously extended to all slaves hereafter born, this Synod would not be understood as excluding those now living from the operation of the benevolent principle above recommended: they believe there may be, at the present time, many slaves belonging to members of the Presbyterian communion, whose situations would be greatly improved by emancipation; and that many others, especially of the children and youth, might be prepared for freedom by the use of reasonable efforts on the part of their masters. But it is difficult to provide by general rules for such individual cases, and this Synod thinks it best to leave them to the operation of the Christian law of love on the consciences of men.

"For the purpose of promoting harmony and concert of action on this important subject, the Synod do

"*Resolve*—That a committee of ten be appointed to consist of an equal number of ministers and elders whose duty it shall be to digest and propose a plan for the moral and religious instruction of our slaves, and for their future emancipation; and to report such plan to the several Presbyteries within the bounds of this Synod, for their consideration and approval.—Yeas 56, Nays 8, Non-liquet 7.

"*Resolved, further*—That this Synod have unabated confidence in the scheme of African Colonization, and hope of its great usefulness, and and that we look upon it as one interesting door of hope, opened to us in the providence of God, for doing a signal service of patriotism to our common country,—an act of justice to the unfortunate African race among us, and for spreading the blessings of civilization, and the everlasting Gospel in the interior of the continent of Africa."

Note H.

On the vexed question of the sin of slavery, I would only say, that the *system of American slavery* has the essential attributes of guilt. Now what is the precise share of guilt that should be assigned to all concerned in upholding it, it is difficult to say. Perhaps some degree of guilt may be assigned to some of the slaves who tamely neglect to qualify themselves for liberty by the use of their limited opportunities for improvement; another share should be assigned to those owners who neglect the moral and intellectual improvement of the slaves; another share should be assigned to those, who, in the capacity of legislators, pass cruel laws on the subject, or who neglect to legislate for the benefit of the slave, whether in the General or the State Governments. Another share should be assigned to those who, though they have the power to influence public opinion in favor of the abolition of slavery, either neglect to employ their influence, or employ it for riveting more firmly the fetters of the slave. On this point I have been pleased with some remarks of Robert Hall, in an Address on the subject of West India Slavery, which he delivered in 1823:

"Slavery, considered as a perpetual state, is as incapable of vindication as the trade in slaves: they are integral parts of the same system, and in point of moral estimate must stand or fall together. If it be unjust to sell men into slavery who are guilty of no crime, it must be equally so to retain them in that state; the last act of injustice is but the sequel and completion of the first. If the natives of Africa were originally despoiled of their freedom by rapine and violence, no man is entitled to avail himself of the condition to which they are reduced, by compelling them to labor for his benefit; nor is it less evident that they could not possibly transmit the forfeiture to their children of those rights which they never forfeited for themselves. Thus it appears that the claim of the planters to hold their negroes in perpetual bondage is vitiated in its *origin;* and having commenced in an act of injustice, can never acquire the sanction of right.

"But here we are most anxious to guard against the misrepresentation of our sentiments. Convinced as we are that negro slavery is most iniquitous in its origin, most mischievous in its effects, and diametrically opposite to the genius of Christianity and of the British Constitution, we are yet far from proposing a sudden revolution. Universal experience shows, that in the body politic, no less than in the natural, inveterate diseases admit only of a slow and gradual cure; and we should deprecate an immediate emancipation almost as much as the planters themselves, from a full conviction that the debasing operation of slavery long continued disqualifies its subjects from performing the functions and enjoying the immunities of a free citizen."

Printed by Libri Plureos GmbH in Hamburg, Germany